Legal Disclaimer

Table of Contents

FORWARD

I want to thank you very much for purchasing **MS Word Legal – *Awareness Explosion*** Volume 3 with an additional BONUS in the back!. This book represents an additional portion of the 6 years of articles that I have contributed to various blogs. I have a first and second volume that is already on both Kindle and Create Space. If you liked volume 1 and 2 then you will also appreciate this volume as well. Volume 3 is an array of situations that will save you hours and hours of frustrating time trying to figure out solutions. We have already been through the scenarios and you will certainly appreciate the effort. These books give you a window into working in a top-tier legal word processing center. This book will go over a tremendous amount of material as well. Each article is very different from the previous and this book covers a lot of ground in an easy to understand format. Whether you work in a law firm or not, you will greatly benefit from this book.

After looking at the articles produced as a whole, I realized, that so much ground has been covered that I saw the need to release it to the public. This book can be used as a study guide for people trying to get into the legal business, to increase the awareness of those working within a legal environment and to give others such as job agency people and those working for single practitioners and smaller offices, a good feel of the day to day interactions and subject matter encountered within a large law firm. I found that blogs move very fast in that an article that I write today will be way down the line and out of sight within a few days and in some cases a few hours. Nevertheless, the information that I touch upon is vital and important and through the medium of self publishing, I can reach and help an exponential amount of people.

There are a lot of technical books on the market, but few that capture the essence of this niche market and the real feel of what goes on in a law firm from day to day. If you take the time to go through all the articles that are taken from the original posts, you will surely increase your knowledge base and level of understanding without a doubt.

I write the articles I do because I see too much generic talk and wanted to make sure that people deal with and see what really goes on from day to day the good and sometimes stressful. Think of this series as a great expansion of your knowledge base. Feel free to follow me on Twitter @legaltestready. I am also an instructor of the great AdvanceTo Training and Consulting. (www.advanceto.com) Through that site you can contact us for basic-advanced Legal MS Word Training. We do public training, test creation, course development for legal firms large and small with our style of training.

Best regards,

Louis

MS WORD LEGAL *AWARENESS EXPLOSION* Vol 3

Articles That Increase Your Ms Word Knowledge Base

How To Affect How Your Documents Open.

I looked into this which resulted in the solution in the forum link I provided below, because of an incident during one of my classes.

I was attempting to show one of my students the **Open and Repair function**. As you know, in order to use this, while in MS Word, you go to File, Open and browse for the file that you wish to run the Open and Repair feature.

When you find the file, you click on the document 1X to select it then you click on the down arrow on the right side of the Open button and select Open and Repair.

But, the student could not do that because as soon as she clicked the file, it **immediately** opened up and prevented her from using the Open and Repair feature. The link below will show you how to change the options in the Folder Menu so that the file allows you to select it and does not react and open from one click.

I would rather not have the one click selection because it limits my control over the document. If there is a problem with the document where someone sent you a virus or you want to run, like we tried, an Open and Repair, not being able to select the file places you at a disadvantage.

This gives you more control over the document, and in our situation here having the ability to **first select a file** without it immediately opening is an option that is necessary.

Check out the link below on how to affect the opening of files.

http://www.sevenforums.com/tutorials/295-folder-options-open.html

......*

Copying All Tables to a New Document

In a great tip from Allen Wyatt who is a great source of info, I thought that in a situation where time was of the essence, this would be great to know.

You might have the need to use the tables in another document or you wanted to work on the tables separately (Updating them) while someone else worked on the textual aspect of a large document.

A macro will do the trick. It will extract all of the tables and in between each one, it will place a blank line.

Under the Developer Tab go to "Macros", Create a name (Copy Tables) and insert the macro text in the Visual Basic Portion that opens up.

If your Developer Tab is not active then you do the following:

1.   For 2007- Click on the Microsoft Word Button, Go To Word Options, Choose Popular and place a check under "Show Developer Tab in the Ribbon"

2.   For 2010 and above, go to File, Options, Choose Customize Ribbon, look for the Choice of Main Tabs, click the Developer Tab and you should now see it listed on your main screen.

Copy this Macro Text and put it in a safe place:

```
Sub CopyTables ( )
Dim Source As Document
Dim Target As Document
Dim tbl As Table
```

```
Dim tr As Range
Set Source = ActiveDocument
Set Target = Documents.Add
For Each tbl In Source.Tables
 Set tr = Target.Range
 tr.Collapse wdCollapseEnd
 tr.FormattedText = tbl.Range.FormattedText
 tr.Collapse wdCollapseEnd
 tr.Text = vbCrLf
 Next
End Sub
```

Give it a try when you can.

......*

Know Where Your Cursor Is When Creating New Styles:

A very common problem is not taking note of where the cursor is before the creation of a style.

While it is true that all new styles should be based on the style "Normal" which amounts to a clean slate, both operators and secretaries alike sometimes forget to select the "**Based On Normal**" selection when creating the new style. Instead they create a style while sitting within another style.

A good example is this common error:

Scenario: The document is making use of the style separator on the second level (Heading 2)

The Second Level is 1.01 style of numbering. The operator notices that each successive paragraph is coming out 1.01, 1.03, 1.05, 1.07 and this also occurs when the TOC is generated. The non-numbered paragraphs are simply body text and are not the problem. So, how was this Heading 2 number skipping situation corrected?

1.   As you know, when using the style separator, the text that sits after the style separator uses a body text style which serves to disassociate the remainder of the paragraph from the Heading 2 text that shares that same paragraph.

2.   The error occurred when creating the body text style that would be used on the remainder of the Heading 2 paragraph.

3.   When the Body Text Style was created, the operator forgot to select Style based on "Normal". Instead, they left the selection as Style based on "Heading 2" which was where the cursor was sitting when the operator created the new style. (Within the boundaries of a Heading 2 paragraph).

4.   By making this error, when the Body Text (which was named Remainder of Paragraph) was applied it acted in effect as an additional Heading 2

thus causing each new additional Heading 2 paragraph to come in as 1.01, 1.03, 1.05, 1.07 etc.

5.   This was easily fixed by modifying the Body Text style (Named "Remainder of Paragraph"), and changing the setting Style Based On "Heading 2" to Style Based On "Normal". This immediately remedied the situation and the Heading 2 paragraphs now numbered as expected 1.01, 1.02, 1.03 etc.

It is very simple to remember that each new style that you create should be based on Normal.

Not realizing this can cause strange behavior where you may not understand the source of the problem but you still experience the time lost and frustration in trying to figure it out.

Resetting Your Keyboard Back To Its Original Settings

Scenario:

This will help whether you are at work or at home. So you sit down at a work station and when you use a standard shortcut key such as Control R (align right) it gives you something else other than what was expected. So in this case, instead of aligning a piece of text to the extreme right of the screen, it pastes in a signature block.

Most of the time this is due to people doing a Macro and using a standard shortcut key combination to activate their macro.

When doing Macros, you really want to use a key combination that does not "interfere" with the existing well known short cut key combinations.

Nevertheless, in some cases you end up in a situation where the PC is not operating in a recognizable fashion due to someone re-assigning well known short-cut keys to other procedures. The question becomes how do we set the keyboard back to the original settings so the PC reacts in a way we are used to.

1.   Display the **Word Options** dialog box. In Word 2007 click the Office button and then click Word Options. In Word 2010-16 display the File tab of the ribbon and then click Options.

2.   At the left of the dialog box Click the Customize button (Word 2007) or the Customize Ribbon button (Word 2010-16).

3.   Word displays the **Customize Keyboard Dialog Box**.

Click on the "**Reset All**" button. (**NOTE:** This button is only available if you've previously made customizations to the keyboard shortcuts.)

4. Word displays a dialog box asking if you want to remove all your shortcut key definitions.

Click on Yes. Word removes all the user-defined shortcut keys, returning them to their default condition.

Click on Close to back out of the Customize Keyboard dialog box.

Click on Cancel to back out of the Word Options dialog box.

It should be noted that in smaller firms, multiple people using the same workstation can experience the above. You may wish to relegate one particular workstation that makes use of the unorthodox keyboard shortcuts so you don't affect other users.

The question in larger firms that make use of individual log-ins, resulting in individual desktops that appear on the screen as a result of a particular log-in is how they react to the changing of keyboard shortcuts.

Depending on how the firm sets up their system, if one user changes his/her keyboard shortcuts and then logs out the new user who logs in may not experience those changes. But the opposite can be true as well meaning someone logs in, changes some of the generic keyboard shortcuts which take effect on the local hard drive of that particular workstation and are then experienced by the next user to log in at that particular workstation.

The next time you use a short cut key and you receive a something totally unexpected instead, you will now know how to restore your keyboard back to its recognizable form.

......*

Get It Done While Your Table Is Highlighted

I guess I should explain the title of this post.

When you need to do a Financial Table within an MS Word Document from scratch, there are a lot of things you can initially do to get the table ready for use so let's go over them.

1. Determine how many columns and rows are needed for your table.

2. Create your table

3. If in Print Layout View, you can select your entire table by clicking on the target symbol that comes up on the top left side of the table when your cursor is within your table.

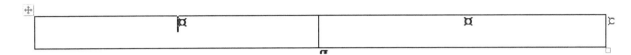

4.   Once your entire table is selected, you can do the following in preparation while the table is selected.

A.   Remove your border lines so that you are left with your grey grid. You can get to this from going to your "Table Tools" button and under "Borders" select **"No Border"**.

B.   Remove before and after spacing so that there is no extraneous spacing in the table.

C.   Adjust the font size if necessary. If you have a wide left hand column or long numbers you may want to shrink the size of the font of the table down to 8 or 9 pitch.

D.   Make sure all cells are bottom aligned. You can get to this under Table Tools under your "Layout Tab" and then look for **left aligned bottom** as shown in the picture below.

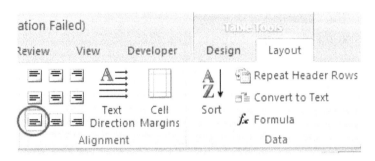

E.   Make sure that those cells that will accommodate your numbers are all Left Aligned. By doing this, you can use the method for your numbers that uses the right tab ⌐ for your $ sign lines in the ruler and the decimal align tab ⌐ for your non-dollar sign lines in the ruler. It won't work unless the cells are left aligned.

F.   Finally, with the Table still highlighted, go into Table Properties and decide on the horizontal alignment. Will your table be left, center or right aligned?

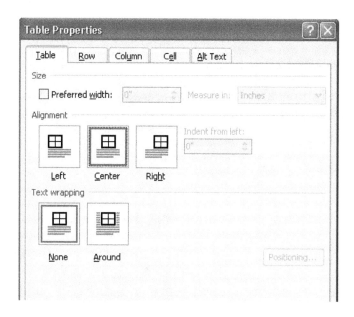

Now you should be ready to put your table together. While there may be minor adjustments to be done with column width etc. this initial exercise that I have suggested you go through, will help you to put your table together a bit easier.

......*

Two Shortcuts Related To Extended Highlighting:

I have talked about the useful extended highlighting feature a number of times. Before 2007, you would use the F8 key to turn it on or the "**Ext**" area of the status bar that no longer exits to turn it on or off.

From 2007 onward, you can still use F8 to turn Extended Highlighting on but now you would use the "**Selection Mode**" in the Status Bar in order to easily turn it off or to know that the function is active.

Either way, when you use Extended Highlighting, you can target specific areas of text for quick highlighting such as pressing the return key to highlight a paragraph at a time or another example would be pressing the period key to highlight a sentence. When using F8 (Selection Mode in Your Status Bar), it highlights up to the first instance of **WHATEVER KEY OR COMBO OF KEYS YOU TYPE**.

But, there are two very good shortcuts closely associated with Extended Highlighting.

1.   **Alt and Left Click:** Lets you highlight a vertical column of text at a time, meaning as small as a character width wide or more "vertically". So you can highlight text vertically without "involving the entire line of text or entire paragraph".

A. A. The contract

B. B. The company

C. C. The Residence

D. D. The Lease

Look at the example above. It shows a scenario whereby a Heading Level has been applied but the original hard coded text is still in place and needs to be removed (referring to the second set of repeated letters).

Use **Alt and Left Click** to go down vertically from A-D and then across 2 characters before you press delete to remove the hard coded A,B,C.D.

2.   You can also use **Control Shift F8** in order to do the same thing (meaning **activating vertical highlighting**), but in order to go down the list vertically you use the **South Cursor Control Key** to move downward and the **East Cursor Control Key** to sweep across the letter and the period (A., Etc.) whereby you would then press delete. Much faster than having to delete each separate letter and period 1 by 1.

Try them both. Two very good short-Cuts from the top-tier.

Changing The Hyperlink Text Color Within A PowerPoint Theme.

The other day, I had to create a mock website using Power Point, I was using 2010. Within the mock site, I needed to Hyperlink everything within the Power Point document so that the mock site would act like the actual site.

If you don't have experience, and have not had the need to change the textual color of Hyperlinks, then you definitely want to know this so that you will never be in a time sensitive situation where you need to change the textual color of a hyperlink in a Power Point slide and you have someone right there waiting.

1. It should be noted that when setting hyperlinks within the PowerPoint document, that is to say links that are not leaving the document to go elsewhere, you make use of the "**Bookmarks Selection**".

2. As I went through the document, I made decisions as to hyperlinking entire pictures and/or shapes that people can click on vs. hyperlinking text so that people can click on a textual item to be taken to another slide within the same Power Point document.

3. So let's see how to change the color of the textual hyperlink within a particular PowerPoint Theme.

Step 1

Click on the "**Design tab**" and find the theme you are currently using and select it.

Step 2

Click "Colors" (right side) and then select "**Create New Theme Colors.**" A popup window appears, that displays the particular color settings of the theme you are currently using.

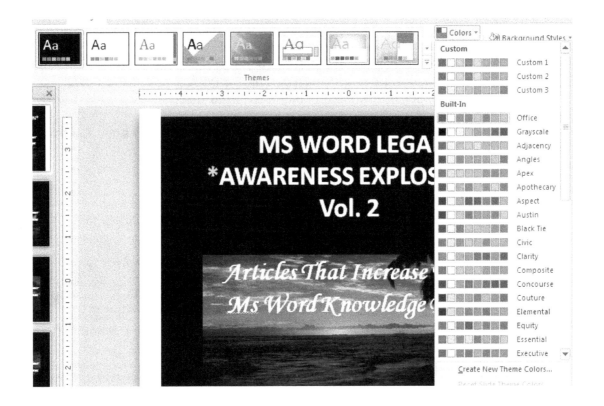

Step 3

Change the "**Hyperlink**" and "**Followed Hyperlink**" colors if you wish to use followed colors. At the bottom of the **Create New Theme Colors** pop-up window, you'll see two selections labeled "**Hyperlink**" and "**Followed Hyperlink**." If you'd like to change the color that the hyperlink turns once it has been visited "selected", click the box beside "Followed Hyperlink" and select a new color there as well.

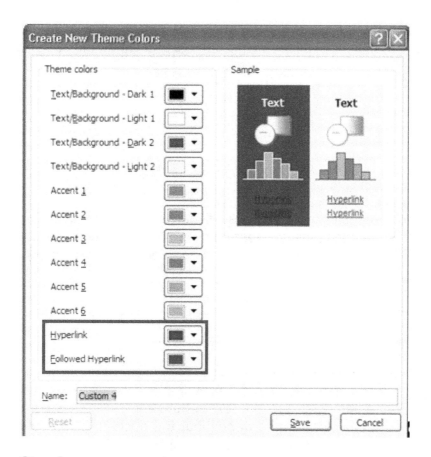

Step 4

Once you save and exit the Create New Theme Colors Dialog Box, if you do not see the Hyperlink text change over to your new color, click on your theme under design and that will update the computer memory and your new choices will kick in.

I suggest you go through this process at least once so if it comes up, you will say I have done this before!

......*

Now My Zoom Feature is Gone:

As you know, if you are working in a big firm, most probably all of your work station settings are tied into your log-on. No one else but you changes anything.

But, for some of you, this is not the case. You sit down at a work station possibly as a temporary employee and you are the recipient of whatever is going on at that particular work station.

So, if you find that the Zoom and Zoom Slider which are vital are not present on the bottom right of your screen above your status bar, you simply **right click on** your **status bar** and place a check next to **Zoom** (which shows your viewing percentage) and **Zoom Slider** that allows you to enlarge and shrink the screen size.

Under the **View Tab**, you can get to the Zoom feature, but certainly not as convenient as having it active on the screen.

I would also on a regular basis, make sure that you also turn on 1. Formatted Page Number (what is the auto page number on a particular page), 2. Section (what Section is my cursor presently in) and 3. Page Number (For Example, 2 of 10). These will supply you with vital info as you go about your work.

......*

Stripping Direct Character Formatting and Some Considerations:

This article is a bit different because it is not the typical clean-up article where you strip everything down to raw text and start all over. Rather, this is about having a situation where someone has either brought text in from somewhere else or through direct formatting used a different font so throughout the document you have areas where the font is different even though it is a word or two here and there it is still noticeable. The document as a whole does not need to be stripped so here are some pointers concerning this scenario.

1.   We may have a situation in the document where throughout the document there could be bolded, underscored and Italicized text that was not done by a character style nevertheless it needs to be left alone. This is important because this means that you can't make "wholesale use" of **Control Spacebar** that strips all direct formatting off of the text. If applied to a particular piece of text (by highlighting) then the rest of the text remains unaffected and it is an effective way to remove instances of fonts that don't match the intended font of the document.

2.   You would want to use the **Control Spacebar** carefully (highlight particular areas to get rid of unwanted fonts) so that the bolding, underscore and italic instances that are wanted by the attorney are not disturbed. So, this means that you don't want to do **Control A** then **Control Spacebar**. Rather you want to go piece by piece.

3.   If you do decide to use **Control A** and Control Spacebar to strip all instances of direct formatting, then you better have a hard copy printout of the document, so that you can ensure that you can reproduce those areas of the document that were bolded, underscored or Italicized that you need to redo.

4.   Before stripping direct formatting from a document, you always want to have examined the document for legitimate uses of direct formatting so we don't get

rid of attributes that the attorney did not want disturbed or removed. Remember, you always have the ability to create a character style so that all of your attributes applied to your text do not have to be direct formatting.

......*

Borders Applied To Paragraph

Many of you seasoned operators and secretaries will find this basic but I assure you that many people don't make the connection when doing tables.

Scenario: You have a number of headings across the top of the financial chart. Each heading is underscored or you have totals or subtotals across the page single or double underscored.

In either event, the Borders and Shading Dialog Box should be utilized to produce the underscore, but many times people (especially newer students and some operators) will associate the lines to the Cell which then causes the following:

1.   Even though the line is associated with each separate heading of each separate cell, when you view the document in Print Preview or you print out the document, the separate underscored headings will appear as one solid continuous line since this feature puts the line from end to end in the cell.

2.   People then try to remedy this by inserting narrow "buffer columns" that have no underscore associated with them but serve to make sure that the underscores that are beneath the Titles or Numbers are visually separated from the underscore of the next column.

3.   While this is a remedy, it is totally unnecessary because all they needed to do was to apply the **underscore** or **double underscore** to "Paragraph" when underscoring Titles or Numbers in a table using Borders and Shading.

4.   By associating the underscore to "**Paragraph**" for your titles and numbers when using Borders and Shading, this feature leaves a bit of room (as shown below in the headings "December 31, 2003 and 2002) on the left and right of each cell it is applied to. So, when you view the table or print it out, there is a clear separation between the columns and no buffer columns are necessary.

ANNUITY AND LIFE RE (HOLDINGS), LTD
CONSOLIDATED BALANCE SHEETS
(U.S. dollars)

Assets	December 31, 2003 (unaudited)	December 31, 2002
Cash and cash equivalents	$ 80,068,310	$ 152,930,908
Fixed Income Investments	117,812,445	153,415,429
Funds withheld at interest	667,824,819	1,427,993,380
Accrued investment income	1,491,179	2,141,338
Receivable for reinsurance ceded	88,480,745	93,6689,173
Other reinsurance receivables	4,580,745	25,025,453
Deferred policy acquisition costs	68,942,628	187,913,648
Other assets	682,050	2,508,858
Total Assets	$ 1,029,882,,339	$ 2,044,698,187

Try it yourself. It works first time and every time. If you are taking a test and you have a financial type table in the test, they will be looking for your use of applying the underscore to paragraph.

......*

Secondary Style Overrides Initial Style of Same Paragraph For "After Spacing".

Scenario:

This issue just came up the other day. For those of you that use a Third Party Software such as MacPac and/or Soft Wise for your Multi-Level Outlines this is not really an issue for you. But, for those of you that use generic MS Word to generate your Multilevel Outlines, then you will find this both interesting and you will gain additional knowledge if this same scenario should arise for you at work or on a test:

The scenario was the following:

We were dealing with a four level Multi-Level Outline. Level Two took the form of:

1.1 → Heading Text ¶ Paragraph Text Paragraph Text Paragraph Text Paragraph Text Paragraph Text. ¶
¶

For "**most**" of the Level Two paragraphs, they shared the paragraph with the text and therefore we had to make use of the "Style Separator" (as shown in red above), and we then applied a Body Text Style to the remainder of the level two paragraph after the Heading material.

The remainder of the paragraph (the Body Text Style), used Justification, Single Spacing and 12 Pts. After.

So what's the problem? Well, while **most** of the Level Two Headings shared the paragraph with the text, there were a number of Heading 2 paragraphs in the document that **did not share** the paragraph and took this form:

1.1   Heading Text

Paragraph Text Paragraph Text Paragraph Text Paragraph Text. Paragraph Text Paragraph Text Paragraph Text Paragraph Text Paragraph Text Paragraph Text Paragraph Text Paragraph Text Paragraph Text Paragraph Text Paragraph Text Paragraph Text.

The question then became when we have Heading Two material on a line by itself, how do we ensure that there is 12 Pts. After Spacing?

If you remember, in the first scenario, we placed the 12 Pts. After in the "**Body Text portion**" and "**not**" in the Heading 2 portion.

What we needed to do was to place **12 Pts. After** in the Heading 2 style as well. In the Heading 2 paragraphs that share the paragraph with Body Text, the "12 Pts. After" in the Body Text will take over for those paragraphs. But, for those paragraphs that have Heading 2 **on a line by itself**, the 12 Pts. After Spacing that we placed in the Heading 2 Style will ensure that there is 12 Pts. of space between the Heading that sits on a line by itself and the paragraph that follows.

......*

Multilevel Outline Problem With Combo Type Number

I like these articles because they help add to people's awareness level and serves as 1 more thing that you have been exposed to.

Here is the scenario of the event:

Operator calls and explains they are attempting to do what I call a "Combo" number in a Multi-Level Outline for Heading 2. The number for Heading 2 style will be 1.01 with the word "Section" placed before the outline number. It should also be noted that the first level of the multi-level outline (Heading 1) is Article I where the number is "**ROMAN**".

1.   So, the operator had already brought in the first instance of Heading 1 on the screen and it reads:

ARTICLE I (soft return)
Introduction (Hard Return)

2.   They are now ready for the level two which is the combo number 1.01. It would have the word Section before it. As you know, a combo number is produced by the selection in the Multi-Level Outline Dialog box "**Include Level Number From**" followed by a period and then the current number type (combined) to produce

the 1.01. The operator types in the period between the two levels (the 1 and the 01) as shown in the picture below.

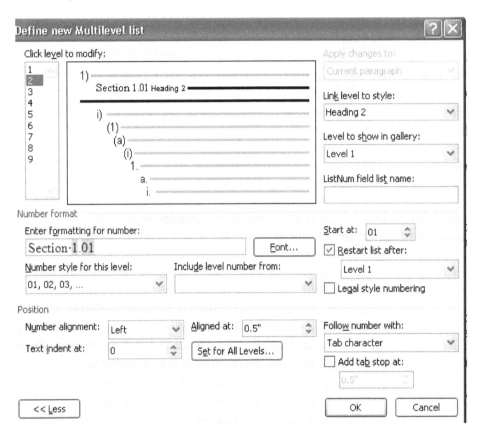

3.   Upon going to "**Include Level Number From**" there was nothing to be selected and it said none. Without the ability to click "**Include Level Number From**" we cannot produce our combo number which is a "combo" of the first two levels.

4.   I asked the operator to please check if in fact level 1 in the multi level dialog box was connected to Heading 1 through the "**Link Level To Style Option**". They confirmed that it was. I had them bail out of the Multilevel Outline Dialog Box and do a save. Upon going back in, still no access to Previous Level Number in Level 2.

5.   Upon going back to level 1, I noticed the lack of grey shading (indicating Field Code) for the Roman number I after the word ARTICLE (as shown in the picture below). This meant that it had to be "**typed**" in instead of produced by going to the selection Numbering type. This now had to be fixed by going to Level 1 and selecting for the Current Numbering Type "Roman I" which when selected turns Grey. The Grey shading tells you it is now set for auto numbering and "**NOT**" typed in manually.

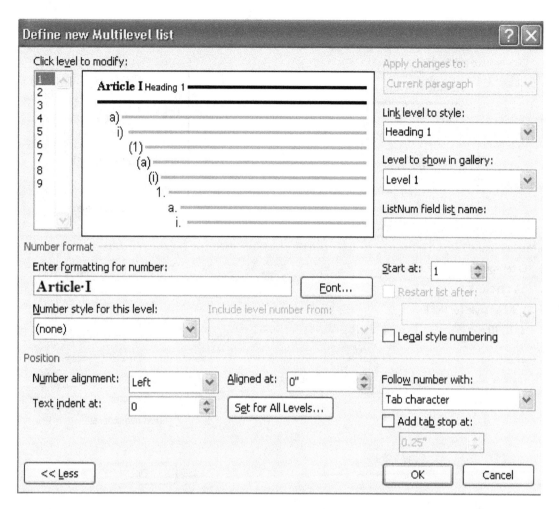

Once the Level 1 was corrected, we are now able to use the "Include Level Number From option" in conjunction with Current Level Number to Produce **I.01**.

6.	Since the first level was a roman number, the combo number will initially come in as **I.01** (Roman.01) but upon selecting "**Legal Style Numbering Selection**" in the multilevel dialog box (**right side**), it then switches over to 1.01.

7.	We did not realize the hard coded roman number error right away because the operator had only brought in the first instance of level 1 and it came in as Article I on the screen "as it should have" so there were no red flags. If done correctly, the Heading 1 should have looked like the picture below. Note that the Roman I is grey shaded. If not then it is hard coded (typed in) and will not work to produce auto numbering.

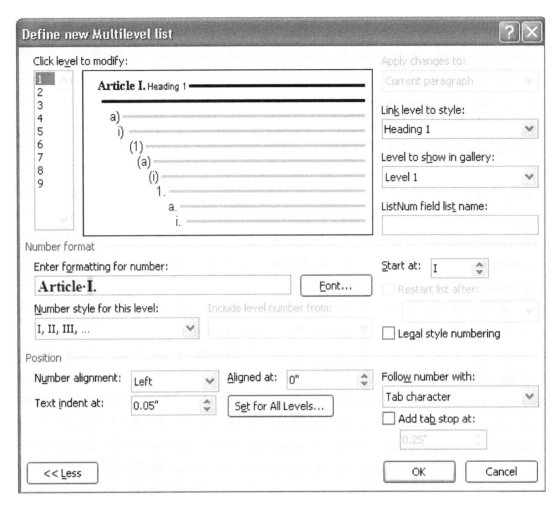

If they had brought in the next major level, Article II, it would have "not" kicked over to "II" since the number was initially "hard coded" (typed in) in the multi level dialog box and would therefore continue to produce the Roman I again and again.

8.   In sum, **do not hard type numbers** in the multi level dialog box. You can hard type parentheses (a), periods 1. and words such as **Article** and **Section** but always make sure the numbers are auto and you use "Number Style for This Level" in order to bring in the Field Codes.

......*

Quick And Easy Deletion Of A Table

This short write-up will provide you with an additional piece of knowledge that is a time saver. It has to do with the deletion of a table.

When working with tables, most people like to work in "Print Layout View" so that they can click on the "Target" symbol as shown below, that appears on the top-left of the table which allows one to select the entire table with 1 click. When in Draft View, there is no target like symbol.

	December 31, 2003	December 31, 2002
Assets	(unaudited)	
Cash and cash equivalents............→............	$ → 80,068,310	$ → 152,930,908
Fixed Income Investments...........→.........	117,812,445	153,415,429
Funds withheld at interest..........→.........	667,824,819	1,427,993,380
Accrued investment income..........→.........	1,491,179	2,141,338
Receivable for reinsurance ceded........→........	88,480,745	93,6689,173
Other reinsurance receivables ....→..........	4,580,745	25,025,453
Deferred policy acquisition costs ....→.........	68,942,628	187,913,648
Other assets...................→.................	682,050	2,508,858
Total Assets	$→ 1,029,882,,339	$ → 2,044,698,187

So, most people when deleting a table, select the table in 1 click and they then use their "Delete" key which knocks out the text of the table and leaves behind the empty grid which still leaves you with having to delete the structure (the empty grid) of the table.

So, we can take care of the deletion of a table with a minimum of 2 clicks.

1.   Place your cursor in your table.

2.   Click on the Target Symbol (top left of table) to select the entire table in 1 click.

3.   Press your Back Space key 1x which will then delete the entire table text and structure.

4.   That is all you need to know!

......*

Affecting Two Basic Shapes Simultaneously

These are tips that I used many times when dealing with shapes when doing cascading text. This is useful for any shapes you are working with.

1   First, if you need to quickly **dupe** a shape you can use **Control D**. That will immediately produce a duplicate shape. If you are duping the shape for purposes of doing Cascading Text (meaning you are using right triangles) then you are going to need to use the flip horizontal feature so that you make sure that the second triangle is facing in towards the first right triangle.

2   Whether you are using right triangles or not and wish to affect both of the shapes " simultaneously" so that making a shape larger, smaller, wider, narrower, the two independent shapes will respond exactly the same if you do the following:

A.   Click on the first shape 1x.

B.   Go to the second shape and do **Shift Click**.

C.   Now whatever you do will affect both shapes simultaneously.

D.   Micro Moving shapes is easy as well. If you need to nudge a shape into place whether it is a text box, (red herring), lines, arrows, ovals etc. you click twice on the lines of the shape and then using your control and directional arrow keys you can micro move the object into place. Up, down, left, right. Give it a try.

......*

Header Row Repeat Is Giving Me Trouble...

Scenario: Header Rows in a number of tables in a document that exceed 1 page are not activating:

When you are in a Table, your "Table Properties Tab" sits at the top of your screen. Within your Table Properties Tab, there is the selection "**Header Rows Repeat**". For whatever reason, selecting the Header Row and checking Header Rows Repeat" was not activating the Header Row.

So, with the Header Row still highlighted, I right clicked my designated header row and went to **Table Properties** and selected under "**Row**" "**Repeat As Header Row At The Top of Each Page**". It then turned on the repeat header feature as expected so there "could" be a glitch in the "Header Row" selection under Table Tools.

With that being said, I ran an "**Open and Repair**" on the document just in case there was any corruption in the Visual Basic aspect of this document and it came up clean.

Adding The Style Separator Icon To Your Quick Access Toolbar.

Just a quick reminder of just what is a Style Separator for those who do not use it often:

In many documents that use Multi Level Outlining, the headings are by themselves and are not part of a regular paragraph. Sometimes, they do share the paragraph and when they do, the majority of the time it is the second level (Heading 2). It would look something like this:

Section 1.1 Provisions of the Contract. Remaining Body Text. Remaining Body Text. Remaining Body Text. Remaining Body Text.

When the Heading 2 shares the paragraph, if we do not put in the Style Separator after the heading material, when we run the Table of Contents it will bring in the entire paragraph into the TOC.

The keyboard shortcut that brings forth the Style Separator is **Control + Alt + Enter**.

The Style Separator Icon is not always available on a particular workstation and if one does not know the short cut keys to produce the style separator, you can waste a lot of time until you get the info.

If you are taking a test at an agency or law firm, this can be a problem since not knowing the shortcut keys and not having the icon available would result in you losing unnecessary points since you could not perform a major task. So, how do we add the Style Separator to your Quick Access Tool Bar?

1.	Right click at the top of your screen and choose Customize Quick Access Toolbar. Your Quick Access Tool Bar has items in it such as Save, Undo, Redo, Open.

2.	After you right click at the top of your screen the Word Options Menu opens up.

3.	You will see "**Popular Commands**" when it first opens. Choose "**All Commands**". Look for "**Style Separator**". Note: In 2003 it used to be "**Insert Style Separator**". Click the "**Add**" Button after selecting **Style Separator** . The Style Separator selection will now appear in your **Quick Access Toolbar**.

4.   The Style Separator (which appears as a small double paragraph symbol) will now be ready for use in your Quick Access Toolbar.

......*

Certain Functions That You Should Know The Keystrokes For When Working On A Workstation other Than Your Own

For those people that temp or those who work in smaller firms where people tend to configure their workstations to their individual liking, you can't always be sure what is available, what is on the Quick Access Tool Bar and what they want you to touch or not to touch.

Here are a few that come to mind to save you time: If you have some others feel free to add them.

F8 (Extended Highlighting) followed by Control End. This will highlight from a specific location to the end of the doc for copy/Move without involving the shell of the document as would happen if you did Control A.

Control Home - Go To Top Of Doc

Control End- Go To End of Doc

Control Alt Enter- Insert Style Separator

Control Shift F8-To highlight a column of text. This will let you take your cursor down and across using your cursor control keys.

Control Shift F9- Strips the field code to plain text such as a completed Table of Contents, Table of Authorities.

Control Shift Spacebar - Insert Hard Space

Control Shift Hyphen - Insert Hard Hyphen

Control Shift N - Strip text to Normal Style.

Control Spacebar- To Strip Direct Formatting off of a paragraph. I should note that you should always use this in piecemeal meaning a couple of paragraphs at most at a time since you can accidentally remove bolding and other attributes that you **wanted** to keep so don't use a Control A (highlight whole document) followed by Control Spacebar approach.

Control Shift C- Control Shift V- Copy and Paste Formatting. Equivalent to clicking the Paint Brush 2x.

CTRL + F3. (Copy Track Changes from One Doc To Another). This will cut the text along with track changes. [Make a backup of the original Word document first before you do this]. Open a new Word document. Press CTRL + SHIFT + F3. This will paste your selected text AND your reviews/track changes along with it.

Shift F3- To Cycle through Change Case selections.

Shift F9- To toggle a field code

F4 - Repeat an action.

......*

1 Click vs. Double Click

To some people this will be very basic and to others it will be very useful.

Some Basics Regarding Paint Brush

1.   I place my cursor in a particular paragraph that has the formatting that I want to share with another paragraph.

2.   If I click on the Paint Brush 1 X and then go to the paragraph that needs that same formatting and click 1x, it will apply the Painted format to the selected paragraph and the paint feature will turn off automatically.

3.   It should be noted, that if I click inside the paragraph that has the formatting I need, click the Paint Brush 1X and then highlight the next 5 or 10 paragraphs that need that same formatting and then lift my finger off the left mouse button it will apply that Painted format automatically to those 5 or 10 paragraphs that I had highlighted and will then turn off.

4.   If I place my cursor in a particular paragraph that has the formatting that I want to share with another paragraph and I double click on the Paintbrush, I can click on paragraph after paragraph without any limit applying that formatting until I am finished applying that formatting to the X number of paragraphs that needed it. To turn off the Paint Brush feature, I can simply press escape.

5.   The Control Key equivalent to the "**double click**" on the Paint Brush is **Control + Shift + C** and **Control + Shift + V**. So, with this method, I place my cursor in a particular paragraph that has the formatting that I want to share with another paragraph(s). I do **Control + Shift + C** and then go to the paragraph(s) that need the formatting and then do **Control + Shift + V**. You can then place your cursor in any paragraph that needs the particular formatting that you had copied and just continue to use **Control + Shift + V** over and over again.

6.   It should be noted that with the **Control + Shift + C** and **Control + Shift + V** method you can grab formatting from one document and apply it to a paragraph in another document. Either way having this knowledge of using the Paint Brush to your full advantage is very valuable. Try it out and you will see how easy it is to use.

......*

Taking Apart The Hourglass: How it Works and Its Equivalent Menu Selections

Some of you are probably scratching your head and saying hourglass?

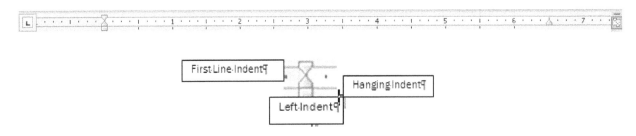

I am of course referring to the left margin of your ruler that contains 3 parts. I will go through all 3 and give you the menu equivalent to each piece. The menu equivalent is very important because if you deal with the hourglass directly, it amounts to direct formatting while modifying a style and dealing with the menu equivalent lends to a more permanent solution as per a style modification. So here we go.

1.	**Bottom Block of the hour glass**. This controls your **Left Indent**. The menu equivalent is **Left Indent** under "Paragraph". Just so you know, at the far side of your ruler you have your right margin which sort of looks like "Home Plate" and its menu equivalent is **Right Indent** under Paragraph.

2.	The **pointing up portion** of your hourglass. This controls The **Hanging Indent** and that refers to the positioning of anything from the 2nd line forward of your paragraph. The menu equivalent is under **Paragraph** under "**Special**" look for **Hanging**.

3.	The **pointing down portion** of your hour glass controls the positioning of the **First Line** of a paragraph. The menu equivalent is found under "Paragraph" look for **First Line** under **Special**.

Great Tip:	When tugging any portion of the hour glass on the ruler, if you hold down your **Alt Key** simultaneously, while positioning an item using any portion of the ruler, you will get a "guide line" which will give you micro control. Give it a try.

......*

TOC With Specific Request...

Scenario: "Heading Two" has the numbering aspect as Section 1.01 (Times New Roman 12) plain text and the textual aspect "The Contract" *Italicized*. When the TOC is generated, the Italicized text within the document does not remain Italicized in the generated TOC. Nevertheless, the attorney wants the TOC to reflect the same look as within the text.

Section 1.01 *The Contract*.

1.	If you are to modify style TOC 2 within the completed TOC and select Italics, then you would affect the entire line "**Section 1.01. The Contract**" instead of **just** "The Contract".

2.	We can create a "Character Style" and apply to the completed TOC the Italic text where needed, but each time the attorney or secretary reruns the TOC, we are back to square one since the directly formatted portions would be overwritten. So, what is the best way to deal with this?

3.	In order to keep the Italicized text and have it also appear within the TOC, the easiest way to deal with this is to **NOT** build the Italicized text into the Textual Aspect of the Heading 2. Instead, use a Character style on the Textual Aspect of each individual Heading 2 portion of text and when you run your TOC your TOC will have the Italicized text in at as requested by the attorney.

4.   For those of you that wish to prevent another person from re-running the TOC we have two choices to make sure no one can run it at a crucial time when we are just about to file the document or send to a client in a certain condition. The two choices are the following:

A.   Highlight the Field Code and do **Control Shift F9** which would strip the field code to just plain text with no visual difference. It will be on the screen as plain text and therefore will visual appear so to another person who most probably will not treat it as a re-generable TOC.

B.   You can also "**Lock**" the Field Code and that will prevent anyone from rerunning the TOC . To do so,

Select the TOC Code you want to lock.

Press **Ctrl+F11**.

When you need to unlock the field, follow these steps:

Select the field you want to unlock.

Press **Ctrl+Shift+F11**

Locking the Field may be the best choice and easiest to do.   You now have a strategy you can use for this type of situation.

......*

Bracket Before The Text Won't Let Me Apply To This Paragraph Only.

Scenario: This happened the other day to a student about to go to a test and this is just the type of issue that does not come up every day, but when it does happen, it can catch you unaware. This is one more scenario to cross off the never ending list:

So, we have a Level 2 (Heading 2) paragraph:

Section   2.1   The Corporate Structure.☐ Remainder   of   Paragraph Text. Remainder of Paragraph Text. Remainder of Paragraph Text. Remainder of Paragraph Text.

We are using a Style Separator after the Heading (The Corporate Structure) and for the remainder of the paragraph we are using a body text.

We are asked to place a Bracket Character ([ ) Before The word "Section" of the Section 2.1.

1.   So we keep our cursor in the Section 2.1 paragraph and under the Home Tab, we go over to the Multi-Level outline button and after choosing the **"Define New Multi-Level List"** we now find ourselves back in our open Multi-Level Dialog Box.

2.   We take our cursor over to the "S" in Section (Within the Multi-Level Outline) and we place a Bracket before the S and then we attempt to apply the Left Bracket to **"This Paragraph Only"**. This option is available on the top right of the Multi-Level Dialog Box. When we go there, it is Greyed Out!!!

3.   Dilemma: If I cannot select "This Paragraph Only", then the bracket would end up giving me the Bracket on Each and Every Paragraph instead of only before the Section 2.1 selection.

4.   Why is it Greyed Out? Well, before my student went to the Multi-Level Dialog Box, they did not take notice where the cursor was. It was laying within the "Body Text Portion" (Past the Style Separator) of the Paragraph and this created a disconnect as to the active Multi-Level Outline.

5.   Once the cursor was placed within the boundaries of the "Heading 2 Material, and we went back into the Multi-Level Dialog Box, the choice to "Apply To This Paragraph Only" was now active and we were able to complete the task. When we are done it should now look like the sample below:

[Section 2.1 <u>The Corporate Structure</u>.□ Remainder of Paragraph Text. Remainder of Paragraph Text. Remainder of Paragraph Text. Remainder of Paragraph Text.]

Know where your cursor is at all times before you do any procedure...

......*

Footnoting Basics Including The Related Styles

Footnote Ref/Footnote Text

This is considered a minor item in the scheme of things until you are in a position of having to change the numbering or text. It comes down to if you are asked to modify Footnotes in terms of their Reference Numbers vs. the actual Footnote text you can waste time figuring it out if you don't know it right off the bat.

You need to know how to modify the actual styles that represent the Footnote numbers vs. the Footnote Text.

1.   You might be in a situation whereby the attorney wanted for whatever reason an alteration to the size of the text. Typically, law firms use Times New Roman 12 for the bulk of the document and the Footnotes are done two point sizes down which gives you Times New Roman 10.

2.   When you insert a Footnote, you end up with a footnote number or a footnote symbol depending on what you choose for the numbering system. You have a Footnote Reference Number within the body of the text which appears Superscripted as well as a corresponding Reference number at the bottom of the page associated with the new footnote.

3.   Pull up your "**Apply Style Toolbar**". That is done by doing **Control Shift S**. If you sweep your cursor over the footnote reference number "within the text" and look at your style window of your Apply Style Toolbar, or your style task pane to the right of your screen, you will see that it reads "**Footnote Reference**". Keep in mind that this is a character style "a" and is not a paragraph style. Therefore, you can (and would only need to) modify its font characteristics and attributes if needed such as bolding, font and font size. This is the name of the style that is associated with the footnote number or symbol.

4.   Now, if you go into print layout and run your cursor over the footnote reference number next to the actual footnote text (at the bottom of your page) the style associated with the footnote number is again "Footnote Reference". If you are to highlight the text of the footnote itself and look at your task pane you will see that the style associated with the footnote text is called "**Footnote Text**".

5.   This is important because if you should have the need to modify the footnote reference numbers or the footnote text in any way, you would know what styles control which parts of the footnote!

6.   Remember, the footnote text tends to be two points below the font of the text of the document. So, if your document is in Times New Roman 12 (a very popular law firm font) then your footnotes should be in Times New Roman 10.

......*

How To Create A Mouseover Screen-Tip With Hyperlink

This is a great little article that allows you to provide "additional pop-up info" concerning text or an image in your document along with a hyperlink that will enable someone to go to another document or website for info or to purchase something.

You can place a phone number or email info in the pop-up. Point being that any info that will place an additional way for people to connect to you or your company is a good thing.

http://www.ehow.com/how_4779622_create-mouseover-microsoft-word.html

......*

On-Line OCR - When You Need To Convert Images To Editable Text On The Go.

In the past, within this forum, I spoke about Zamzar.com which is a free document conversion site. The issue a number of people brought up at the time was their concern for confidentiality. My answer to that is that you might need to convert a document that was not of such a sensitive nature and you used a site such as Zamzar where you could be out and about and still convert a document. Not everyone has the 24/7 services of a major law firm.

Now, in this article, we are talking about being able to OCR a document no matter where you are. Again you may be doing the following:

A.   An attorney downloads a PDF to a smart phone, tablet or laptop. It could be part of the research the attorney is doing.

B.   You don't have Adobe Professional, Nuance or MS Office related OCR capability available at the moment.

C.   You don't have an App to do it.

D.   You are out, maybe in a diner or a place where you just want to be able to get access to the text so that you can make progress drafting a legal document or share that newly available text with another attorney through email.

E.   Maybe you are not that computer savvy, you are outside, your office is not in a position to do it for you at this time, it could be late at night, you could be working for a small firm, and you just want a way to convert a PDF that was originally scanned in on a scanner and needs to be OCR'd right now!

If any of these scenarios fit a possibility for an attorney you work with, you should tell them about **Onlineocr.net**. If you don't sign up, you could upload up to 15 images per hour.

If you sign up for a free account, you can convert multiple PDF documents over to editable text to a number of different languages.

This is good to know about when you need to be able to grab text which minutes before was unavailable to you.

......*

Locking A Field

Scenario:

There is a time sensitive document. It is about to be filed with the court. The TOC, TOA are done and are exactly the way the author/attorney wants it to look. There may have been some manual manipulation or style modification to the TOC and TOA.

Either way, the attorney wants the TOC and TOA locked down while he has paralegals and others giving the document a last look. He does not want someone rerunning these headings without his okay. Get it? That is the scenario. How do we lock the field. And, keep in mind, it does not have to be a law firm per se. It can be any scenario where the author of the document wants to control when a Table of Contents, Table of Authorities, Index of Terms is to be updated.

When you are in a situation where you want to make sure a field does not get updated, or at the very least prevent someone who was not in the loop from doing so, you can accomplish this by locking the field. Locking prevents a field from being updated; the last result (update) stays in place until you unlock the field and then update it if needed. To lock a field, perform these steps:

Select the field you want to lock.

Update the field, if desired, by pressing **Shift+F9**.

Press **Ctrl+F11**.

If you later want to unlock the field, follow these steps:

Select the field you want to unlock.

Press **Ctrl+Shift+F11**

This method is recommended because it is very easy to reverse quickly. This is opposed to the Control Shift F9 method which strips a Field Code down to Plain Text which make the TOC, TOA or Index of Terms no longer capable of being generated.

......*

The Invisible Article 1

This is yet another item to be checked off the list of anomalies that occur within documents:

Scenario: Level Heading 1 Centered

Article 1
Introduction
(Soft Return After Article)
(Hard Return After Introduction) (12 Pts. After)

When Heading 1 was set up using the Multi-Level Outline Dialog Box using the configuration "Article 1" as the numbering aspect, the following occurred:

1.   When Heading 1 was selected from the right side style palate, Heading 1 came in in the following manner:

An Empty Soft Return
Introduction (Hard Return)

There was an empty soft return and the textual aspect of Heading 1. The numbering aspect DID NOT come in.

2.   Thinking we must have overlooked something in the Multi-Level Dialog Box we went back in. Article 1 was in place as it should be and we checked that Level 1 was in fact "Linked" to Heading 1 which it was.

3.   We then went back to the Heading 1 text in the actual document and stripped it back to Normal style (Control Shift N). Then, we reapplied Heading 1 from the right side style pallet. Again, it came in with an empty soft return and the textual aspect of Heading 1.

4.   Again we went back to the Multi-Level Dialog Box. This time we went into the Font Button and the CULPRIT was staring at us. Under Font Color, it read "**No Color**". We switched that over to "**Automatic**" and when we came out of the Multi-Level Dialog box, Article 1 was now visible. Problem solved.

5.   When doing Multi-Level numbering, you must remember that the **Numbering Aspect** of a particular level has its own Font and the **Textual Aspect** has it own Font controlled by the present level Heading you are implementing.

......*

Modify Rather Than Manually Manipulate

So, here is the scenario. Attorney does not like the look of the completed TOC and/or TOA.

What is the problem? The Text of the Table of Contents or Table of Authorities is "**crowding**" the page number of the TOC and/or TOA. The attorney wants you to clean it up so that there is a distinct clear lane between the text and the page number to the extreme right.

Look at the ruler of a completed TOC or TOA. There is a right Tab (Red) sitting all the way to the right. That Tab controls your page numbers generated by the TOC and TOA. The right margin (Blue) sitting in the ruler controls the right margin of the text generated by the TOC and TOA.

Table·Of·Authorities¶

Page¶

Cases¶
Am.·Trade·Partners·v.·A-1·Int'l·Importing·Enterprises,·Ltd.,·757·F.·Supp.·545·(E.D.·Pa.·
    1991)..→..4¶
Am.·Trade,·757·F.·Supp.·at·550 ....→..............................4¶
Am.·Trade,·757·F.·Supp.·at·552 ....→..................................4¶
Bank·of·Vermont·v.·Lyndonville·Sav.·Bank·&·Trust·Co.,·906·F.·Supp.·221,·227·(D.·Vt.·
    1995)..→...5¶
Brouwer·v.·Raffensperger·Hughes·&·Co.,·199·F.3d·961,·967·(7th·Cir.)·(one·must·
    personally·agree·to·be·an·operator·or·manager·of·a·RICO·enterprise·to·face·civil·
    liability),·cert.·denied,·530·U.S.·1243·(2000)..........................→..................5¶
Cincinnati·Ins.·Co.·v.·Hertz·Corp.,·776·F.·Supp.·1235,·1238·(S.D.·Ohio·1991)...........→.............2¶
Dick,·726·F.·Supp.·at·1091 ....→.................................3¶
Hall·Am.·Ctr.·Assocs.·Ltd.·Partnership·v.·Dick,·726·F.·Supp.·1083,·1091·(E.D.·Mich.·   (

1.   The first mistake usually made is people start to tug towards the left the right tab thinking that the tab will affect the text of the TOC and TOA. This will result in your page numbers heading towards your text.

2.	The second mistake happens when people tug the right margin over towards the left which does create a clear lane all the down the TOC and TOA but, as soon as it is regenerated, you are back to square one.

3.	In order to solve it for good, do the following. Either modify TOC 1 or 2 depending on the level that is encroaching on the page numbering and under Modify-Format-Paragraph, make your "Right Indent" 0.5.

4.	For your TOA, modify the style "Table of Authorities" and make your **"Right Indent" 0.5.**

5.	This will ensure that you have a clear lane and it will stay for good.

Try it out next time you run your TOC or TOA

......*

Setting A Document Password vs. Restrict Editing

This write-up will be helpful in clarifying the difference between setting a Password for a document so that the recipient cannot open it without the having the password. This is different from making use of "Restrict Formatting and Editing Mode" which allows the recipient to access the document but having restrictions placed on what can be altered. So let us go over both:

Password Protection:

1.	Go To File, Info "**Protect Document**" Permissions.

2.	Under the "Protect Document" Button, go down to "**Encrypt With Password**".

3.	Type Your Password. Make sure you write it down somewhere. Also, from experience, make sure your fingers are on the proper place on the keyboard because you can type your "password" in wrong 2x and think you typed it in correctly. Then, when someone tries to open it with your "password", it does not work and you and the recipient are locked out and stressed out. It may also be a great idea to save a unencrypted copy of the file as well before you set the password.

As to "**Restrict Editing**" you can get to it from File, Info, Protect Document, Restrict Editing or you can get to it from the Developer Tab as well as the Review Tab.

1.	With Restrict Editing, we use it to lock a document for Fillable Forms, as well as allowing certain types of editing and determining groups and/or individuals that can do so.

2.	When doing Fillable Forms, we restrict the document so that the recipient can only type in the form fields while the text of the document is off limits.

I suggest you familiarize yourself with both scenarios discussed in this article.

......*

Displaying Recent Documents and the Pin Feature

I like to write articles whereby the concept is simple but because you just don't know the remedy, this can cause unnecessary stress:

Let me give you a scenario:

This situation does not have to be a law firm but can happen in any firm:

Attorney says: I need to get into a document right away. They say you worked on it a few hours ago. I don't remember the name, but you worked on it recently so we should see it in your recently edited files. You go to File and there is only 1 file listed. The setting that would show you up to 25 of your recent edited files has to be accessed and bumped up so that your "**Recently Edited**" list displays the all important documents that the attorney was desperate to get into.

Not knowing how to remedy this would place you in a stressful position and would also frustrate the attorney and cause a stressful atmosphere.

So how do we bump up the number of recently edited documents?

1. Click on **File**.

2. Go To **Options**

3. Under Advanced, go the section heading that says "**Display**"

4. Under **Display**, bump up the number of documents that you want to show in your Recently Edited Documents.

Display

Show this number of <u>R</u>ecent Documents:	10
Show <u>m</u>easurements in units of:	Inches
Style ar<u>ea</u> pane width in Draft and Outline views:	1˝

Pins:

You will notice that next to each "**Recently Edited Document**" in the list you will see a Pin like graphic.

That Pin, if clicked, will take that document and will throw it to the top of the list and will make a divider line between the "PINNED" documents and your Recently Edited Documents. The PINNED document will act like a quick access bookmarked file and will not get replaced as do the documents on the "**Recent List**" as documents pile up.

Note: If you want to pin a file not available on the "**Recent Documents**" list, open the file once and close it. It will then be available on the "**Recent Documents**" list.

To **Pin** a Folder:

1.   To **PIN** a folder to the "Open" screen, click "Computer."

2.   Move your mouse over a folder in the list of "Recent Folders" on the right side of the "Open" screen. Click the sideways push pin icon to pin the folder to the "Open" screen.

......*

Some Clarity Regarding Index Of Defined Terms

The goal of this article is not to give you a lesson on defined terms but to clear up a few things:

1.   The Index of Defined Terms always sits after the Table of Authorities if you have one or after the Table of Contents if you do not have a Table of Authorities in a particular document.

2.   Defined terms are designed to allow the author of a document to refer to a company, entity, individual, etc. in a shortened manner. So, if we have for example The New York Board of Education referred to numerous times throughout the document, you would most probably see this organization name defined in the following way: The New York Board of Education ("NYBOE"). Once the entity has been defined after the first use of the full entity name, you can then refer to that entity with the shortened term "NYBOE" for the remainder of the document.

3.   When the defined terms are marked and an Index of Defined Terms is generated, the reader then has a list of all the terms in the document that were defined and the page number showing where the full version of the term was mentioned. The reader is directed to the page where the term was marked and they can then see the full name or term before it was defined (shortened) so they know exactly what the shortened term refers to.

4.   Depending on the attorney, some will ask for the defined terms to be bold. ("Bold Defined Term"). Others will not. If you are asked to Bold all of the defined terms, then you may wish to consider doing so by use of a character style whose only job is to bold text. In this way, if the attorney changes his/her mind you can simply modify the style and remove the bold across the board.

5.   When generating an Index of Defined Terms you can generate it as one column or two columns depending on the length or how many terms are involved. I

have generated Indexes that have 75 - 100 terms where the two column format works great.

6.   If in Draft View, (formally normal), the Index will appear as one long strip even if you generate as two columns. When you switch over to print layout view then you see your two columns.

7.   After you generate your Index of Terms you will notice a "continuous" page break before and after the Index. This is normal and not to be removed. They are part of the Index of Defined Terms set up.

Index·Of·Terms¶

	Page:		Page:
·······Section Break (Continuous)·······		
Compl ·········→········· 1¶		
Complaint ·········→········· 1¶		
RICO ·········→········· 1¶		
·······Section Break (Continuous)·······		
¶ ¶		
·······Section Break (Next Page)·······		

8.   Finally. if you generate a two column Index of Terms and they happen to want the word "Page" positioned over each set of page numbers for each column you can use a one row two column table with the word "Page" at the extreme right of each cell. Remember to remove the lines of the table.

......*

Ghost Entry In The Table of Contents Keeps Haunting Us

Scenario:

Mix in with this time sensitive situation, a boss asking for the document, not knowing, the cause needing to solve the problem nevertheless.

So, we run a Table of Contents. In one area of the TOC, we have an entry.

Whose· On·The·Team..................................40¶

Directly·followed·by:¶

--40¶

1.   With this particular document, we used the "Title" style to produce a 1 level Table of Contents. Each Heading throughout the document used the **"Title"** Style.

2.   Seeing duplicate or strange entries in a TOC is quite common and seeing this strange entry temporarily threw us. Since there was nothing on the entry line in order to help us zone in on what line the document accidentally was using the "Title" style which then caused it to be included in the TOC, it took a little longer to find it.

3.   Because of editing, we had removed some page breaks in order to get rid of some wide gaps of nothingness on a particular page.

4.   When we removed the page break, the first thing on the next page forward was a new Title Heading for a new section of the document.

5.   When we decided to place the page break back in, a hard return was made and then the page break inserted.

6.   When the hard return was made, since it was sitting in the "Title" line, the Hard Return picked up the Title Style and on the screen looked like what you see below:

------Page Break------ (Hard Return) (Title Style)

7.   The Title style on the same line as the Page Break made it more difficult to zone in on what was causing the extra line in the TOC. Placing the cursor on this line immediately saw the cursor jump to the Title Style in the right side panel. Once this line was stripped to Normal (Control Shift N), and the TOC re-run, the problem was resolved.

......*

Using Small Caps

THIS DEED OF NOVATION is dated as of the 19th day of May, 2005 (this "**Deed of Novation**") among ABC Company, a stock life insurance company organized under the laws of the State of New York, United States of America, whose statutory home office is at 200 Park Avenue, New York, NY 10166 ("**ABC Insurance**"); Piggy Bank AG, London Branch, whose registered office is at Winchester House, 1 Great Colt Street, London EC55 52DB, United Kingdom (the "**Relevant Dealer Affiliate**"); and Save Save Global Funding II, a statutory trust organized in series under the laws of the State of Nevada, with respect to Series 2005-9, whose registered office is at c/o AMACAR Pacific Corp., 6525 Morrison Boulevard, Suite 318, Charlotte, North Carolina 28211, United States of America (the "**Issuer**").

WHEREAS, the Issuer, ABC Bank, and Piggy Bank Corp., are parties to an Indenture dated as of May 7, 2002, as supplemented by a first supplemental indenture dated as of May 30, 2003 (as the same may be amended, modified, restated, supplemented and/or replaced from time to time, the "**Indenture**").

WHEREAS, the Issuer, the Relevant Dealer Affiliate and the Dealers named therein are, among others, party to a Dealership Agreement dated June 7, 2002 (as the same may be amended, modified, restated, supplemented and/or replaced from time to time, the "**Dealership Agreement**").

WHEREAS, ABC Insurance, the Relevant Dealer Affiliate and the Issuer are, among others, party to an Indemnification Agreement dated June 7, 2002, as amended by Amendment No. 1 to the Indemnification Agreement dated as of June 4, 2004 (as the same may be amended, modified, restated, supplemented and/or replaced from time to time, the "**Indemnification Agreement**").

Certain documents make use of small caps (as you see above in "**This Deed of Novation**" and "**Whereas**") in the following ways: 1) in the letterhead, 2) as a stylistic look of a way to start off each new paragraph by applying small caps to the first word of each paragraph such as the word Whereas, 3) as a look that is used when companies are mentioned throughout the document and in the signatures and on and on.

When you have the use of Small Caps throughout a document it is a good idea to assign a character style whose sole function is to Small Cap any text that needs to have Small Caps applied.

1.   One thing that occurs often enough is the need to change case when using Small Caps on areas of text that are in Upper Case when Small Caps is initially applied.

2.   When Small Caps is applied to text that is initially in UPPERCASE, there is no apparent change in the text and therefore many an operator will take this as the attempt to apply Small Caps was not successful.

3.   It does not make a difference whether it was applied by use of a Character Style or manually highlighting the text when applying Small Caps.

4.   In order for the Small Caps to properly take effect, the text that is currently in ALL CAPS needs to be switched over to Initial Caps. The text which had

Small Caps applied will then immediately take effect and will now reflect the attribute. And of course, in order to do this, just use Change Case.

5.   Change Case. In 2007-16 under the "Home Tab" you will see the "**Aa**" button towards the left side of the screen.

6.   You can cycle through the different aspects of the change case selection by using **Shift F3** as well as the **Change Case button**.

……*

Character Styles And Two Rules You Need To Know

Here are two scenarios relating to Character Styles which show you how MS Word looks at Paragraph Based Styles vs. everything else.

Scenario No. 1:

Section· 1.01→<u>The· Organization</u>·¶ · Remainder· of· Paragraph.· Remainder· of· Paragraph.· Remainder· of· Paragraph.· Remainder· of· Paragraph.· · Remainder· of· Paragraph.··Remainder·of·Paragraph.··Remainder·of·Paragraph.¶

1.   Above, we see an example of a Heading 2 entry that shares the paragraph. The Textual portion of the Heading 2 paragraph (The Organization) needs to be underscored and because this Heading will be in the TOC, we will need to use a Style Separator.

2.   In order to underscore the Textual Portion of the Heading 2, you will be building the underscore into your Heading 2 style. This will momentarily underscore your entire paragraph until you apply your style separator which will cut the underscore off after the Body Text Style is applied after the Textual Portion of the Heading Text.

3.   If you were to use a Character Style (that underscores text) for the underscored portion, the underscoring will be brought into the TOC while underscoring that is **built into the Heading 2** style **WILL NOT** and that is what you want.

Scenario 2:

(a) → <u>The· Initial· Plan</u>.· Remainder· of· Paragraph.· Remainder· of· Paragraph.· Remainder·of·Paragraph.¶

1.   Above, Heading 3 shares the paragraph. The Textual Portion (The Initial Plan) needs to be underscored.

2.   Heading 3 **will not** be used in the TOC therefore no Style Separator is needed.

3.   If underscore was built into the Textual Aspect of Heading 3, the **entire paragraph** would remain underscored since there is no Style Separator to turn it off after the Heading Text Portion.

4.   In this case, a Character Style is the better choice, since it will only target the selected Heading Text and nothing else. Also, we do not need to concern ourselves with TOC issues since this Heading 3 will most likely never be included in the TOC. If it was to be included, we would simply revert over to the Style Separator routine.

......*

The Status Bar: Section, Page Number and Formatted Page Number

This particular issue comes up at work and with each new student I come across. The issue is the important distinction between **Page Number** and **Formatted Page Number**.

On the bottom of your screen, you have a Status Bar which shows items such as Section, Page Number, Formatted Page Number, Word Count etc. When you right click on the Status Bar, you place a check next to those categories that you want to have displayed at the bottom of your screen. For me, **Section, Page Number** and **Formatted Page Number** are essential.

Customize Status Bar

✓	Formatted Page Number	38
✓	Section	5
✓	Page Number	42 of 54

1.   **Section:**   If I am working in a document with multiple sections, I want the ability to know at a glance, where my cursor is. This is important for changing numbering formats, the layout of a page (Portrait/Landscape) printing a particular section and other section related items where knowing where the cursor is important.

2.   **Page Number:** I have a 50 page document. I am on page 10. At a glance, I want to know how large the document is and what page within the overall file is my cursor presently situated in.

3.   **Formatted Page Number:** I have a 50 page document, I am on page 6 and it is been set to read Page 2 at the bottom of the page. How so? Here is the scenario as to how we get page 6 of the document to read Formatted as "2".

Page 1 of Document - Cover

Page 2 of Document - Table of Contents

Page 3 of Document - Table of Authorities

Page 4 of Document - Index of Terms

Page 5 of Document - First page of the main part of the document.

Page 6 of Document - Second page of the main part of the document Formatted to be numbered as "**2**" on the bottom of the page.

Each time you sit down at a different work station other than your own, check your Status Bar and as a general rule, check your Status Bar each time you start a new document.

Scenario: Heading 1 Centered

Article 1 (Soft return)
Gap
Introduction (Hard return

Article· 1↵

Introduction¶

Above, we have the situation of a Centered Heading 1. Between Article 1 and the "Introduction" line there is a Gap of 1 line which is the look that the author wanted for that level. The question then becomes how do we properly produce the Gap?

1.   The soft return after the Article line enables us to apply the Heading 1 style that will control this level 1x instead of having to apply it 2X if we were to place a hard return on the "Article" line as well as the Introduction line. We want both lines to react immediately from the **one** application of Heading 1.

2.   Some people will use an additional soft return after the Article line in order to produce the gap, but it you were taking a test or you were at work, that would be a red flag that your knowledge base needed to be bolstered.

3.   So, how to properly produce the gap? You produce the gap in the Textual Aspect of Heading 1. You modify Heading 1 and set the Heading for Double Spacing (under Paragraph) and you make sure that Before and After Spacing is set to zero. If you leave 12 PTS after you will get a triple space before each new paragraph.

4.   By setting the Heading for Double Spacing, there is no need for the extra soft return that would have had to be applied by direct formatting throughout the entire document.

5.   Your document will look clean and your document will be totally controlled and automated by styles and not direct formatting.

......*

Uppercase Raw Text And The Effect It Has on Your Completed TOC

This article will be helpful to those who do not understand certain results concerning the look of the finished TOC.

Many issues that affect the finished Table of Contents actually stem from the raw text of the document before any Styles or Multi-Level Outline was activated. Let's go over those items that cause unexpected results in your completed TOC.

1. If a Title is in ALL CAPS in the raw text, then before you apply the Heading Style, I suggest you change that text over to Initial Caps (use your Change Case Button under the Home Tab or Shift F3) and build the ALL Caps aspect into the Heading Style (under Font) if the Heading for a particular level within the document itself requires ALL CAPS.

2. Leaving the raw text in ALL CAPS while also building ALL Caps into your Heading Style, will result in the ALL CAPS in the raw text "overriding" the ALL CAPS attribute in the Heading Style. You then end up with the text of that particular heading being brought into your TOC as ALL CAPS.

3. On the other hand, building ALL CAPS into the Heading Style only and changing the raw text over to Initial Caps before applying the style, results in the TOC having Heading Text in Initial Caps. So, you will only have your ALL CAPS within the document itself such as the text of your Heading 1.

4. Knowing this scenario as described above, allows you to take preventative action if the Headings within your TOC have to be in Initial Caps while certain Headings within the actual document need to be in ALL CAPS.

It should be noted that once your TOC is run, you have control over the modification of the TOC in terms of the positioning of the lines and spacing between the TOC levels by modifying your TOC 1 and TOC 2 styles.

Reminder and Great Tip: If the Heading text of the TOC crowds the page numbering of the completed TOC, then modify TOC 1 or 2 and under Paragraph, place a Right Indent of 0.5. This creates a clear lane between the Heading Text of a particular level and the Page Number as shown below.

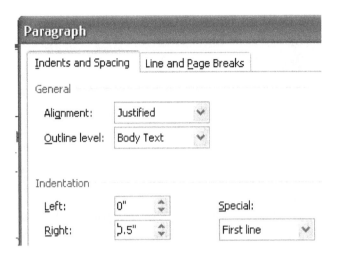

REPLY·MEMORANDUM·OF·LAW·IN·SUPPORT·OF·DEFENDANTS·↵
JOHN·DOE·AND·JOE·SMITH'S·MOTION·TO·↵
DISMISS·COUNTS·FIVE·AND·NINE·OF·THE·ADVERSARY·COMPLAINT¶

¶

....Section Break (Continuous).......................................
Table·Of·Contents¶

Page¶

¶

....Page Break...

......*

Use Of The Change Bars-A Second Set of Eyes

This particular option never ceases to amaze me in terms of the group of people that want the changed lines off and "never to be shown" vs. those that want it used but only on the left, only on the right etc.

As you know, when you run the Document Compare in MS Word or a third party software such as Workshare (formerly Deltaview) or ChangePro you have the option of using Change Bars also known as **Changed Lines.** In MS Word, you can control the feature under the Review Tab and then under The Track Changes Options/Changed Lines.

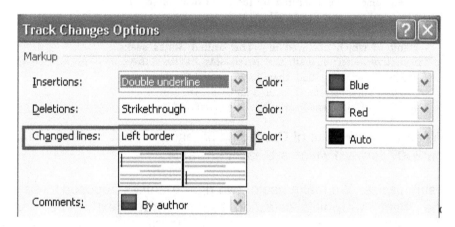

Why is this feature useful? Well, let us say that a paralegal or attorney has the need to go through a 120 page single spaced document in order to check all of the blackline changes that were made by a client or another attorney.

Now let us suppose that on one of the 120 pages, a comma was changed or a number was changed on a particular page and nothing else was touched on that page. Without the Change Bar, the likelihood of you seeing that blackline change is low. But, if you have a Change Bar sitting to left or right then you are being alerted that indeed, there was a change made on the page no matter how small a change it is.

So, you can see how this feature can be a very important 2nd set of eyes when scanning through a document for blackline changes made. I believe it is to the advantage of the attorney to make use of it. Look for it under the Review Tab and then under "The Track Changes Options/Changed Lines" as shown above.

This Court has jurisdiction over this action pursuant to 28 U.S.C. §§ 1331, 1345, and 1355(a).This Court has venue in this matter pursuant to 28 U.S.C. §§ 1391(b), (c), and 1395(a).Plaintiff, the United States of America, seeks civil penalties and injunctive relief against the defendants, Icon Health & Fitness, Inc. ("Icon"), Wal-Mart Stores, Inc. ("Wal-Mart"), Sam's East, Inc., and Sam's West, Inc., for failing to give the Consumer Product Safety Commission ("CPSC" or "the Commission") timely notice of defective products that could create substantial product hazards and of products posing unreasonable risks of serious injury to consumers. Specifically, the United States seeks civil penalties because the defendants failed to report a dangerous defect and unreasonable risk of injury in exercise equipment manufactured by Icon and distributed by Wal-Mart, Sam's East, and Sam's West, even after these companies had been notified of dozens of injuries caused by the equipment -- many of which occurred in . The United States seeks injunctive relief against the defendants because they continue to deny that they have any obligation to report such defects, risks, and injuries. Wal-Mart's, Sam's East's, and Sam's West's own stores¶

We don't always make use of Cascading paragraphs, but issues have cropped up from version 2007 forward which are easily solvable.

Just to summarize. We make use of **two right triangles opposed to each other** along with the "**tight**" wrapping selection under "**Wrap Text**". The Cascading Paragraph will usually appear on the cover page of a Preliminary Prospectus. Thanks to Christine of AdvanceTo for pointing out the fix to me:

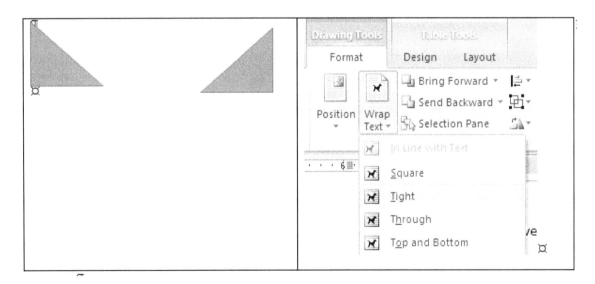

1.   If you are working in an MS Word 97-2003 saved doc, then the routine we have always made use of works fine.

2.   When you are doing this same procedure as a "Word" doc, (2007 on Docx) there is a bleed effect of the Cascading text into the right side portion of the right triangle of the Cascading Paragraph. It will not take the proper shape on the right

side. The left side seems to always be unaffected. Manipulating the right side (right triangle) will not stop the problem and it can be both frustrating and time consuming.

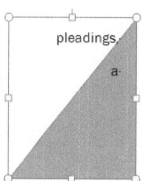

Perhaps because he recognizes the defects in his the Trustee chooses not to address the allegations contained within the Complaint, but instead introduces plethora of new "facts" that are outside the Complaint and without support. The Trustee's resort to this improper and prejudicial tactic demonstrates just how insufficiently pleaded the allegations of RICO and fraud are against John Doe and Joe Smith, and clearly shows that both counts should be dismissed as to them¶

3.   When the text starts appearing in the right side "right triangle" you do the following: We are assuming that you have already applied Wrap Text "Tight" to the two opposing right triangles.

A.   Select the right side "right triangle" by itself.

B.   **Right Click** and go to **Wrap Text** and choose "**Edit Wrap Points**".

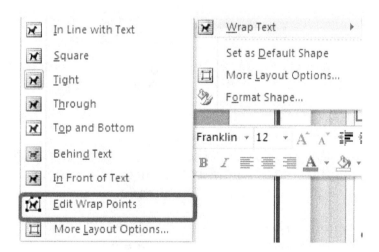

C.   When you click on "**Edit Wrap Points**", you simply tug on the points until they lay directly on the intended shape. Make sure the Wrap Points **mimic the shape** of the right triangle. So when it is done, you are looking at your right triangle with the "Edit Points" taking on the shape of the right side "right triangle".

D.   The text of the Cascading Paragraph will now take on the intended effect (V Shape) on both the left and right side as expected.

Perhaps because he recognizes the defects in his pleadings, the
Trustee chooses not to address the allegations contained within the
Complaint, but instead introduces a plethora of new "facts" that are
outside the Complaint and without support. The Trustee's resort
to this improper and prejudicial tactic demonstrates just how
insufficiently pleaded the allegations of RICO and fraud are
against John Doe and Joe Smith, and clearly shows that
both counts should be dismissed as to them

This is another one of those items that if you don't know the fix it could cause an unnecessary stressful situation. And just so you know. The very last thing to do when using Cascading text is to select both triangles and making the color white. If you should select "No Color" the shape will collapse.

Give it a try when you can.

......*

MS Word Go-Back Command

Scenario: You are working on a very heavy markup. You know the type. If you take your eye off of the screen it is difficult just to find where you made the last edit.

You may also be working on a heavy edit laden document where you are asked to do something else with this same document for the attorney. You are already fatigued and the going back and picking up where you left off is just tedious. So this short-cut lets the system do the location finding of where you made your last edit and helps to save the wear and tear on your eyes.

When editing, **Shift+F5** goes back to up to three editing points, and when you press it for a fourth time, it will then return to where you started with your cursor. When you open a document, it only "remembers" the last editing point.

......*

The Roman and The Combo Number

This is sure a weird title huh. Well it is important that the concept is explained especially for those new to Multilevel Outline Numbering.

Scenario:

Heading 1

ARTICLE I (Roman I) (soft return)
INTRODUCTION (hard return)

Heading 2

Section 1.01 The Company (hard return)

So, we set up Article I in the Multi-Level Dialog Box where the Numbering Aspect of Level 1 is the word Article followed by a Roman I.

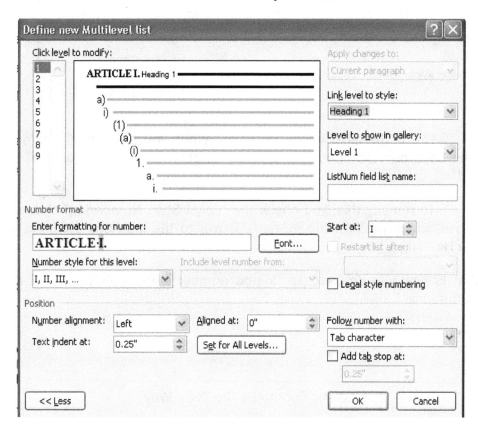

For Heading 2 we see that we have a "Combo" number. The number is 1.01. A Combo number "**which is what I call it**" is composed of the first and second levels brought together to produce the end result of 1.01 in the Multi-Level Dialog Box.

1.	Combo numbers are created by going to "**Include Level Number From**" and choosing "**Level 1**" followed by a period and then you going to "**Number Style For This Level**" and choosing as in our example above, the **01, 02, 03** style of numbering.

2.	When the two pieces come together, you get your 1.01 or 1.1. depending on the needs of the document. Both pieces will be Grey meaning that they are automated and not hard coded (typed in).

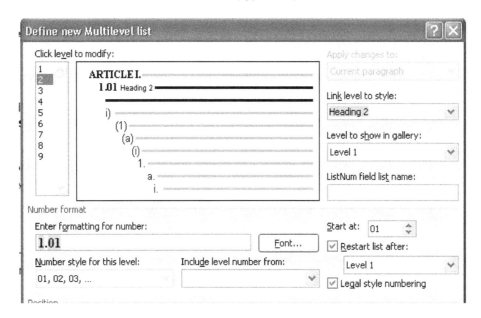

3.	This is the most important point. When your Heading 1 has a Roman Number as does our example, your Combo number will initially come in as I.01 (Roman.01).

4.	To remedy this, you check the "**Legal Style Numbering**" check box as shown above, which will turn the Roman.01 over to the intended 1.01 but will not disturb the Heading 1 Level.

That is how you deal with a Combo number when your first level is using Roman numbering.

Give it a try

Editing Footnotes The Right Way

There are situations whereby people will alter the footnote material with Direct Formatting. Let's review the way to affect the look of the Numbering Aspect of a Footnote and/or the Textual Aspect of a Footnote.

Modifying the styles that represent the Footnote numbers vs. the Footnote Text.

1.   Suppose the attorney wanted an alteration to the size of the Text or the look of the Text or Reference Number. .

2.   When you insert a Footnote, you have a Footnote Reference Number within the body of the text Superscripted as well as a corresponding Reference number at the bottom of the page associated with the brand new footnote.

3.   Sweep your cursor over the footnote reference number "within the text" or at the open Footnote at the bottom of your page, your style pane to the right will read "**Footnote Reference**".

4.   Now place your cursor on the footnote text. The style associated with the footnote text is called "**Footnote Text**".

5.   If you need to modify the footnote reference numbers or the footnote text in any way, you now know what styles control the two parts of the footnote!

6.   Do not alter the numbering or the text of the footnote with direct formatting. It only causes additional work for someone who has to fix up the mess.

......*

Dealing With Footnote Separator Lines:

Scenario:

You need to alter the spacing after the Footnote Separator Line. They request that the footnote separator line, have 0.6 After Spacing between the Separator Line and the first line of the first Footnote.

The Key thing: "**Draft View**" You cannot get to the Separator Lines for editing purposes from **Print Layout View.**

1.   Go to Draft View.

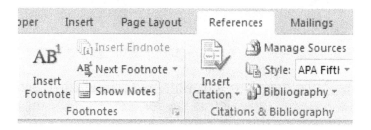

2.   Go to References, choose Show Notes.

3.   Click on down arrow next to Footnote Separator Line.

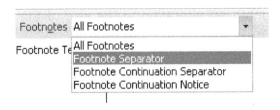

4.   Now you can enter your Footnote separator. Go to your Home Tab and Paragraph and put in the 0.6 After Spacing. **Close** the open Separator Line area (click on "X" to the right) and you are good to go. By putting in 0.6 after, you can guarantee that the first footnote of every page will not lay right on top of the footnote separator line.

Determining The Width of Your Columns When Doing Tables

When doing financial tables in a legal environment, they come in all shapes and sizes. Some portrait, some landscape. Some have top headings while some have top and side headings.

The focus of this short write-up is how to know the exact width of your columns that contain your numbers when doing financial tables.

1.   As you may already know. we use lines applied to "Paragraph" under Borders and Shading when we underscore the sub totals and totals as well as the Headings. The underscore applied to Paragraph will leave some space on the left and right of the cell as shown below. If you have two columns of numbers side by side then that space becomes essential in order to delineate between the two consecutive columns in terms of the underscore. If you use lines applied to "cell" then the line goes from end to end of the cell and although you have separate columns, the lines will take on the appearance of 1 long unbroken line.

	December 31, 2003	December 31, 2002
Assets	(unaudited)	

2.   So, what does this have to do with column width? When we underscore the numbers in a financial table, let us say for a sub total, if the column width is correct, then it should look like the below example if we used lines applied to Paragraph.

Sub Total: _____ 675,987.00

3.   The above example shows the line before the number but no extension of the line after the number. This means your column is perfectly sized.

4.   If you see this:

Sub Total: _____675,987.00_____

Then you instantly know that your column width is too large because there should be no excess line **after** the number .

5.   If you have excess line simply go up to your ruler and tug the column over toward the left and your excess line will disappear from the right side.

When you see the table looking like example 2, you now will automatically know the problem and the remedy.

......*

The Connection Between The Numbering and Textual Aspect Of A Multi-Level Outline.

This article will highlight an error that is sometimes made with those new to Multi-Level Outlining.

1.   When we first start a new Multi-Level Outline, the first thing we do is to Link the first 4-5 levels in the Multi-Level Outline Dialog Box to the corresponding Heading Levels in the "Link Level To" section of the Dialog box.

2.   We then take care of the Numbering Type and the positioning of the outline number. The "**Aligned At**" section controls the first line of the outline heading while "**Text Indent at**" controls the position of the second line forward of the heading if there is a second line.

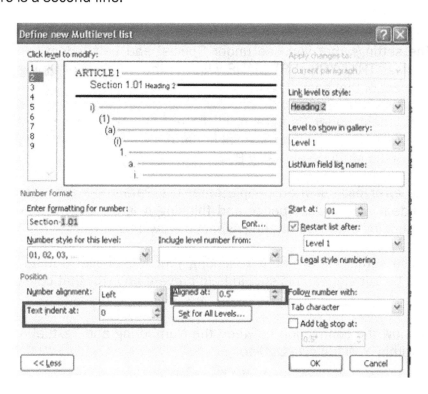

3.   We then turn our attention to the Textual Aspect of the heading level we are working on and take care of those items such as line spacing, before/after spacing and alignment (such as left or justified).

4.   When modifying the Textual Aspect of the Heading Level and entering Paragraph under Format, upon doing so, you most probably will see settings under Special and Left Indent and this is where the problem begins.

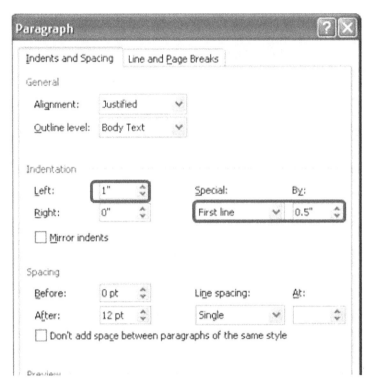

5.   The settings that you see under Special and Left Indent are merely reflecting the settings **THAT YOU JUST MADE** when in the Multi-Level Dialog Box for the Numbering Aspect of that same level.

6.   Left Indent under Paragraph, is the equivalent of "Aligned At" in the Multi-Level Dialog Box. Hanging under Special under the Paragraph Tab is equivalent to "Text Indent At" in the Multi-Level Dialog Box.

7.   The error occurs when people enter the Paragraph Tab see settings under the Left Indent and under Special and thinking it is an error remove those settings. The positioning of the Numbering Aspect then will collapse.

8.   Those settings are merely reflecting your Multi-Level Outline position settings and must be left alone. This should help prevent an error that causes much frustration.

Now you know the connection between the Numbering and Textual Aspect of a Heading Level within a Multi-Level Outline.

......*

I Delete It and Here It Is Again...

Scenario: I was asked to remove a Table of Contents ("TOC") which was generated right after the cover page of a document. The Table of Contents as you know, is a Field Code. Before I deleted the Table of Contents, I was asked to capture the TOC as a JPG which I did using the wonderful Snag-it software. They no longer wanted the TOC to have the ability to update and wanted a picture instead, to represent the final TOC before the piece was published. At this point I have a picture of the Table of Contents on the TOC page. With me so far?

1.   Keep in mind that in order to deactivate the field code, instead of outright removing it as I did in this present example, I could have a) used **Control Shift F9** to strip the field attribute and render it plain text and/or b) locking the TOC field with **Control F11** which would prevent any further update to the TOC which would have solved the request of no further updates.

2.   So I save the MS Word file as a PDF and upon creation of the PDF, my TOC page has the JPG of the TOC followed by the actual TOC which I "thought" I deleted earlier.

3.   When I deleted the TOC, I should have also stripped any empty returns back to normal (Control Shift N) or highlighted any empty returns and deleted them.

4.   What caused the TOC to reappear was the setting under File-Options-Display-Printing Options-"Update Fields Before Printing".

Printing options

- [✓] Print drawings created in Word ⓘ
- [✓] Print background colors and images
- [ ] Print document properties
- [ ] Print hidden text
- [✓] Update fields before printing
- [ ] Update linked data before printing

5.   When I saved the MS Word Doc to a PDF, the system looked at the conversion to PDF as **"Printing To PDF"** and updated any fields in the document including the TOC which technically was still active due to the empty returns that were not properly dealt with which is why the deleted TOC "reappeared." Removing that setting would of course prevent field codes from automatically updating each time you go to print or convert to PDF. Simple Fix if you happen to know it. You do now.

......*

Turn Off The Preview If You Wish To See The Whole Style Name:

You will understand the value of this shortly. It is a common scenario:

For starters, before I format (style) a document, I place myself in "Draft View" which lets me see the Style Tracking paragraph by paragraph on the left side.

I also open the right side style panel (under Home-Styles-Little Box To The Right) and under options (at the bottom of the panel), I ask for All Styles (my particular preference) and ask for Alphabetical as to how the styles are displayed.

So here is the scenario:

Scenario: Secretary was asked to use "**Signature**" style which is generic to the style pallet. When selected, it places your cursor at 3.0 on the ruler and you can then set up your signature.

1.   The secretary was telling her boss there is no such style and he kept saying yes there is and both were becoming increasingly agitated. She just kept repeating that she could not find it.

2.   So, when we set up styles and start to use multi-level outlining and other styles, the positioning of your styles will be reflected on your style pallet to the right. In terms of the Signature style, it comes in at 3.0 on the ruler as shown below. When it is shown on the Pallet it will be barely visible on the extreme right if you have the "Preview" button checked at the bottom of the style pallet.

3.   The secretary not knowing to turn off the Preview selection and not taking the time to expand the size of the style pallet would indeed have trouble initially spotting the signature style. Once the Preview has been turned off, then all of the available styles will be clearly visible since they will be lined up neatly on the left hand side of the Pallet as shown above.

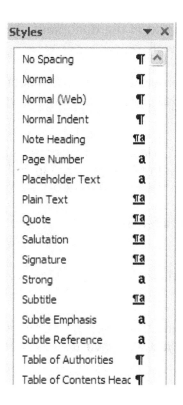

4.   If you like using the Preview, there is nothing to stop you from turning the Preview Function off or on as needed.

5.   Make sure you familiarize yourself with the Style Pallet and Preview Function. Keep in mind that if a Style Name is long and you remove the Preview check then you may not see the left side of the Style Name unless you widen the right side Style Pallet window. Knowing how the system reacts when you have the Preview on or off is valuable.

......*

Table of Contents With Specific Request Revisited.

Scenario: "Heading 2 of a legal document. The Numbering Aspect is 1.01 Times New Roman 12 Regular) and the Textual Aspect of Heading 2 "The Contract" (Italicized). Heading 2 also shares the paragraph with body text and therefore makes use of the Style Separator as shown below.

1.01 → *The·Contract.*·Remainder·of·paragraph·remainder·of·paragraph·remainder·of·paragraph·remainder·of·paragraph·remainder·of·paragraph·remainder·of·paragraph·remainder·of·paragraph·remainder·of·paragraph·remainder·of·paragraph.¶

When the TOC is generated, the Italicized text built into the Textual Aspect of Heading 2 style is **NOT** replicated in the TOC. Nevertheless, the attorney in this case, wants the TOC to reflect the same look as within the text of the document. Meaning, the Textual Aspect of the TOC should be Italicized as well.

1.   If we modify style TOC 2 within the "completed" TOC and select Italics, under "Font", then you would affect the entire "Heading 2, instead of just "The Contract" which is the Textual Aspect of Heading 2.

2.   To accommodate, create a Character Style that Italicizes and apply it directly to the Textual Aspect of each individual Heading 2 entry instead of building Italics into the Textual Aspect of the Heading itself.

3.   When the TOC is generated, the Character Style that was applied will come into the TOC as requested.

4.   Some might say, why can't I just Italicize those portions that need Italics after I run the TOC directly on the TOC text?

5.   **Answer:** If you should apply Italics directly to certain portions of the completed TOC then each time you rerun the TOC, you will have to re-do the direct formatting italics each time.

Summary:

A.   If you build attributes such as Bold, Italics and Underscore into the Heading Styles then it will not be carried over to the TOC. This is the norm.

B.   But, if you apply those same attributes directly to the text or by use of a Character Style, to each individual Heading, it will be carried over to the TOC. For special requests such as discussed, you now know how to properly accommodate.

Conclusion

So we made it to the end of Volume 3 of Awareness Explosion! Do you realize that if you have bought all 3 books, you would have been exposed to 150 high level scenarios with solutions and full explanation? This is quite a package and it is designed to take your awareness level skyward.

Working in a Legal WP environment takes knowledge, exposure to different scenarios and problems and that is what enables you to grow. I believe that this series will continue as long as I am writing and will serve to help those of you that are new to the game, coming up the ranks and want the knowledge now!

Please feel free to contact us at louis@advanceto.com, louisellman@gmail.com for courses and/or training, testing and grading services. Join us on LinkedIn under the group AdvanceTo Legal and Corporate Word Processing Training Forum.

Best regards,

Louis

STYLE TYPES

Don't let this chapter fool you in terms of thinking that you are getting a lesson on Styles. Our beginner class is devoted to Styles. We spend 4.5-5 hours on this class alone. If you are in need of a styles class, contact us at **888-422-0692 Ext. 2** or email me at louisellman@gmail.com or louis@advanceto.com. It does not matter where you reside. We do great phone and internet classes. We also have a nice booklet that goes through a letter from start to finish and describes each piece as to styles. At the end of the booklet, the entire letter is styled from beginning to end. What I do want to do with this short chapter is to make sure that you are clear in terms of **style types**. Some of you will already know this and many of you will have never bothered to notice this at all. So, let's look at the **Right Side** Style Palate.

1. Under the **Home Tab**, Click on the little square box to the right of styles.

2. Your right side style panel opens up. Go to **Options** at the bottom right hand side of the panel and choose "**All Styles**" under Select styles to show.

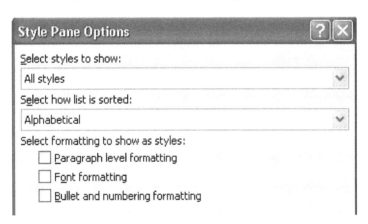

3. The Paragraph Style: As shown below, if you look to the right of the style "Body Text Justified" you will see a paragraph symbol. That let's you know that you are dealing with a "**Paragraph Style**". A Paragraph Style affects the entire paragraph and it will show up in the left side style area when you are in Draft View. You can modify a Paragraph style by either **Double Clicking** on the style name in the left side panel or **Right clicking** on the style name in the right side panel.

4. The Character Style: Unlike the Paragraph Style, a Character Style **only** affects the text that you **highlight and apply the Character Style to**. A Character Style

will add a particular attribute such as **Bold**, <u>Underscore</u>, *Italic* etc. To the right of the Character Style you will see a small "a" such as you see below.

5.   **Why would we use this**? Many times when we do Defined terms within a legal document such as ("**NYSE**") the defined term for the New York Stock Exchange, there are times when we are asked to **Bold** all of the Defined Terms. So, if there are let us say **70 defined terms** and we have bolded each one manually and then we are at some point told to "unbold" them, it can be a cumbersome process since **we may not be able to wholesale remove the bolding** since **other parts** of the document **are bolded as well** so we may be forced to unbold them 1 by 1. If we would have used a Character Style on **each of the Defined Terms**, we could have easily modified the Character Style and **removed** the **bolding** whereby after Modification, the bolding would **instantly be removed** from **all** Defined Terms entries.

6.   When you create a Character Style, you go to the button at the bottom of your right side panel and **Create a New Style**.

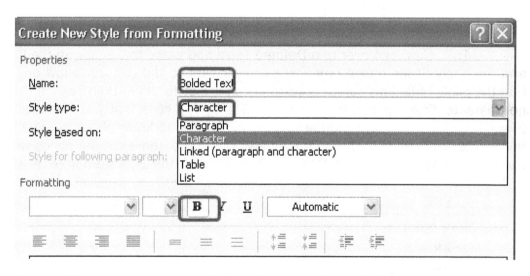

7.   Name the **Character Style**, make sure you choose the style type "**Character**" and then **activate the attribute** that you will be attaching to the Character Style (in this scenario **Bold**).

8.   When you need to apply the Character Style, **highlight the piece of text you wish to apply the Character Style to** and click on the **Character Style** name that is sitting in your right side panel.

9.   **Note:** The **Character Style** unlike your **Paragraph Style,** will not show up in your Left Side Panel. Only Paragraph Styles show up in the Left Side Panel in

Draft view. Important: If you have a scenario such as the one I described above where we needed to **Bold** Defined Terms or any other item where you needed to bold but could be asked to "unbold", I would always create a Character style **devoted** to that situation. So, with the Defined Terms situation, I would make a Character Style that is named **Defined Terms Bold**. In this way, if I choose to apply Bold Character Styles to a number of different items, I could modify one style **without affecting** those other items that also needed to be bolded. On the other hand, if you use the same Character Style for a number of different scenarios, then if you need to wholesale remove bolding from one situation, you end up removing the Bolding from **all situations** and that would not be helpful. In sum, if you use Character Styles **create a separate Character Style for each different scenario** that you utilize it for.

10   How can I tell if a **Character Style** has been applied to text? By just looking at the text, it would **not be apparent** that a **Character Style** has been applied. If you have a crowded right side style pane you may not see it either. I have an easy way for you to do this. Press **Control Shift S** and your Apply Styles Dialog Box comes up. In the picture below, I had my cursor in the text of the paragraph that **did not involve** any bolding or other attributes and it simply shows I am currently in a paragraph with a Body Text style applied called **Body Text 0.5 SJ** as shown below. For those who are curious, **SJ** stands for **Single** and **Justified**.

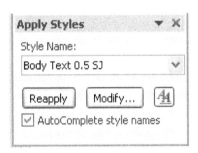

11.   Now, I go over to a **Defined Term** and place my cursor on the **Bold** text and my **Apply Styles dialog box** now switches over to the picture below and shows that the piece of text my cursor is **currently on** is a style called Bold Text. If there was **no Character Style applied** to the text, the **Paragraph style** that you see listed above (Body Text 0.5 SJ) **would continue to show**. It is good to know about the Apply Styles box. **Note:** You can type the names of styles and the names of the styles will come up for you to select and also note that you can **Modify** the style **from here** as well.

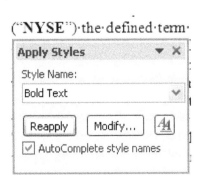

12.   The Linked Style. An example of what a Linked Style symbol looks like is shown below.

Plain Text

13.   **So what is a Linked Style**? With a Linked Style, if you apply the style to a paragraph then the formatting (**Tabs, before/after, line spacing, alignment, fonts etc.**) will be applied to the **entire** paragraph. But, with the Linked Style, if you should **highlight a piece of text** and apply that **exact same style**, only the **text attributes** would be applied to the highlighted piece of text.

14.   When you create a new style and want to make a Linked Style, you will find the setting as you see in the picture below.

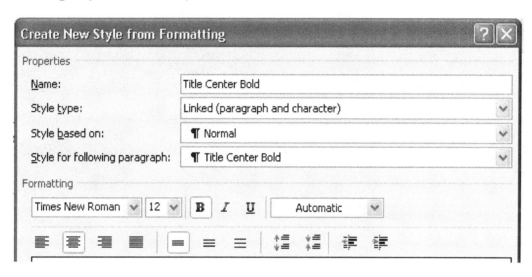

15.   When I apply **this particular style** to text, it **Centers and Bolds** the line. When I **highlight a piece of text** and apply the Character aspect of this Linked Style, it would simply **Bold** the text.

16.   Finally, if you need to **disable** the Linked Styles at any time, you simply check the "Disable Linked Styles" (as shown below) and the style will then act solely as a Paragraph Style.

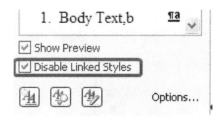

The End